A GUIDE
TO SECURING
A JOB

Even in a recession!

Antonio De Maria

The Key to Achieving Is Following a Proven Method & Pathway To Success

This resource has been compiled from information from numerous sources and years of personal experience on the part of the author and I thank the many people who have supported the compilation of this program.

Antonio De Maria B. App. Science, RN, Certificate 4 Trainer, Assessor

Editing and Layout by Antonio De Maria
Published by Antonio De Maria
Written and Illustrated by A. De Maria 2014 Bangkok, Thailand.
First Published 2008, Reviewed and Reproduced, 2012.
©A.DE MARIA 2015 Bangkok

The author and Chief Editor is Antonio De Maria, who has worked in the front line services in this field for over 28 years. Tony is the founder, a past CEO and Director of the **Enable Group,** a Company providing Rehabilitation, Training and Recruitment, committed to promoting a skilled workforce. He has worked in the Age Care and Disability Sector since 1978, in a number of roles, including Developmental Educator, Case Manager, Staff Training Officer, University Lecturer, Human Resource Manager, Registered Nurse, Therapist, and Advocate, for a variety of government and non government agencies. He has a Bachelor of Applied Science (Developmental Disability) and is a Nationally Accredited Vocational Trainer and Assessor. Tony has had a long-term commitment to Disability and Aged Care Sector reforms and Advocacy, and has committed **Enable Learning Guides** to continue this work. The proceeds of these resources contribute to continuing research and development in the industry.

From the Author *Antonio De Maria*
B App. Science (Disabilities) Cert 4 Workplace Training, Registered Nurse

This book provides a series of educational sessions **designed to train you** to get work as a care worker, in many areas off community services such as aged care, disability services and many others.

This book is a compilation of over 30 years of work I personally have been involved in. I have personally applied for many jobs and assisted many students in successfully getting work. It's not hard if you follow some key principles.

CONTENTS

WHO IS THIS FOR?   8

INTRODUCTION   10

WHAT TO EXPECT FROM THIS RESOURCE   12

PREPARATION FOR JOB HUNTING   14

BUILDING CONFIDENCE   17

IDENTIFYING YOUR SKILLS   18

A CARE-WORKER   21

A HOSPITALITY WORKER   23

AN OFFICE WORKER   26

COMPETENCIES & BASIC SKILLS YOU WILL NEED   29

THERE'S MORE THAN ONE WAY TO GET WORK   35

WHAT TO DO WHEN APPLYING FOR WORK   42

WHAT TO DO DURING A DOWNTURN OR RECESSION   45

WRITTEN APPLICATIONS   49

RESUME PREPARATION   56

THE NEXT   58

STEP   58

THE PURPOSE OF A RESUME   60
    WHY MUST IT LOOK GOOD 60
    IS ONE RESUME ENOUGH? 60
    WHAT DOES A RESUME CONTAIN? 61

REFEREES AND REFERENCES   63

THE INTERVIEW   78

KEY PRINCIPLES OF WORKPLACE DRESS CODE   83

EMPLOYMENT OPPORTUNITIES   86

APPENDIX / NOTES   97

Who is this for?

This is an excellent resource for the job seeker and an equally valuable tool for those who are considering strengthening their position in case they are laid off.

This is a working tool for
- Employment and other vocational preparation professionals such as, Job Network Providers (JNP), Vocational Rehabilitation Providers, and other employment support personnel.
- Secondary School teachers involved in employment preparation activities.
- The jobseeker

Don't let all the hype about a recession spook you into a state of panic. By revising your tactics to include a more solution-centred approach to employers, you stand a better chance of getting hired in today's difficult economy.

Unemployment numbers may well continue to head in the wrong direction this year, and for 2015 isn't going easy, either.

So knowing that, what are you going to do about it?
- If you are **a job seeker** what must you do personally?
- If your job is to get others work, **what is your duty to others** who rely on you?
- Are you going to **take control,** make your own breaks, and create opportunities where others see none?

A lot of people are worried about their jobs or lack of job but aren't taking any action because they often don't know what to do. Some think there's nothing they can do.

You can either believe you have no options, or you can do some digging and uncover them.

It takes focus, work, planning, and you need to be willing to adapt, to learn, and to get creative. You've got to develop a sense of resiliency. You need to change your perception; with resiliency, you can recognize opportunities where others may only see bad situations.

Above all, you need to start somewhere, and then persevere even when adversity is staring you in the face. This resource is an excellent starting point for the job seeker.

Consider all the things over which you have control rather than focusing on those about which you can do nothing. You may be surprised how much influence you have over your circumstances - you really can make your own luck.

The best recession-proof jobs are those that are least sensitive to economic downturn, and which have the highest combined scores for pay, projected workforce growth, and number of openings.

Protect your Present Job
Before you venture out to look for new jobs or those that will hold on during a recession it is best to try to protect your present job first.

Where are the Jobs - Jobs that are "Recession-Proof"
If you are searching for recession-proof jobs, then consider:

- **Health care** continued to expand in over the past 12 months, health care has added many jobs.

- **Education and community services** is steady with some positive increases over the past year.

INTRODUCTION

The purpose of this BOOK is to assist you in getting a job if you have not worked before or are re-entering the workforce.

There are many different industries where employers are continuously looking for workers, for example, jobs are frequently available in –

- Hospitality
- Care work
- Tourism
- Fruit picking (seasonal)
- Office Work
- Cleaning
- Mining Industry
- Security Services
- Police Services

The bulk of work in Hospitality, Care Work and Office Work is in large towns or city centres and suburbs, however there are many jobs available in country areas if you know where to look and who to ask. Cleaning workers are in constant demand.

There is a high demand for skilled workers with many jobs available across Australia. This booklet is designed to assist you with getting one of them.

As you may also be aware the demand for labour does at times outstrip the availability of ready and willing workers so often industries turn to securing migrant labour because they are short of staff.

WHAT MAKES A VALUABLE EMPLOYEE?

Anybody who is genuinely **committed** to meeting the needs of a potential employer will stand out when applying for a position as the best skill to have when presenting for any position is a GOOD ATTITUDE.

The main area where there is considerable work is in Hospitality, which includes;
- **Restaurants**
- **Hotels**
- **Motels**
- **Holiday resorts**

These positions require you to have a high standard of personal presentation, excellent communication skills and a well-developed knowledge of customer service. As the Hospitality industry works closely with Tourism, it is also an advantage to have good local knowledge and access to information about upcoming events.
On the occasions when you may not be able to assist a customer, they will not mind if you maintain a pleasant ATTITUDE. That will be what they remember, not the fact that the information needed was not available.

You must be honest, trustworthy, flexible, friendly and know how to be a good communicator.

You need to be **flexible** in the hours you make yourself **available** for employment and remember that many businesses now operate seven days a week every day of the year. The majority of the labour demand, however tends to be from 7 am to 10 p.m.
In the beginning you will find that work is usually available on a casual basis, however there are many opportunities for experienced and appropriately skilled workers to secure a permanent position either part time or full time.

TO BE A GOOD EMPLOYEE YOU MUST HAVE

- **the right Attitude**

- **the right Skills**

- **the right Knowledge**

WHAT TO EXPECT FROM THIS RESOURCE

This book will help you to identify your current skills and how to make the most of them. There is an exercise to assist you in conducting a "Skills Audit" (p. 14), which will give you a clear picture of where your strengths lie and what you can genuinely offer a potential employer.

You will be guided to identify a number of employers and I will help you write a resume following our guide, and prepare yourself for an interview.

Knowing your particular abilities and being able to talk about them gives you more confidence. Your chances of getting a job are greatly increased when you can tell employers just what you **CAN** do and what you are particularly **GOOD** at doing.

Most importantly we will focus on the skills you require to gain employment

PREPARATION FOR JOB HUNTING

PREPARATION FOR JOB HUNTING

CHECKLIST FOR JOB HUNTING	Yes	No
HAVE YOU ;		
* identified your skills, abilities and past achievements		
* identified your preferences for worksites		
* thought about and defined your preferred work-lifestyle		
* written notes which summarize your experience of work and education		
* identified the work environment you would like		
* researched at least three path possibilities [e.g. hospitality, aged care, production work]		
* talked to people working in the field you are targeting		
* identified the relevant positions you are considering		
* identified employers or people relevant to your career choice		
* an understanding of the different approaches used to obtain interviews		
* identified additional skills		
* obtained your past employer references		
* prepared an appropriate resume and practiced writing cover letters		
* studied the interview process using relevant books, audiotapes or a counsellor		
* identified relevant employment services		
* reasonable alternatives in mind if initially unable to get your first choice		
* talked over your alternatives with the significant people in your life		

 **Activity**

What do you have to do next?

BUILDING CONFIDENCE

This is an area often overlooked but has proven to be an essential part of job hunting, particularly for the long-term unemployed. There are various approaches to achieving this goal and it will depend on the individual as to find what works for you. Here are a few suggestions you may not have previously thought of. Take the time to find your own methods if these are not appropriate for you, as it will be obvious to any prospective employer when your confidence is lacking –

- exercise daily and make it really physical
- join a group of similar interest
- complete an unfinished task
- develop a support network with at least 5 friends and relatives
- list your good qualities
- take on study or volunteer work

(Handy Resources for Surviving Unemployment, A useful guide for workers p.22)

RE-ESTABISHING A ROUTINE

It can be difficult to maintain the discipline of a daily routine when you are unemployed and your time is not linked to a schedule or deadline. Punctuality and effective time management are two essential qualities that an employer will look for when recruiting new staff members, so here are some useful points for you to consider to establish a regular routine:

- get the daily paper or use the free ones at the library
- groom every morning, have a shower, brush your hair and clean your teeth
- try making your appointments in the morning and always turn up at least 10 minutes early
- set regular times for meals everyday and stick to them
- go for a daily walk at a set time or start an exercise routine
- never leave your dirty dishes; always wash them up after each meal

(Handy Resources for Surviving Unemployment, "Establishing a Routine" p.23).

IDENTIFYING YOUR SKILLS

IDENTIFYING YOUR SKILLS

Skills audit

The **skills** and **knowledge** you have at present can be listed separately under these two headings as shown below.   Draw up a similar list for yourself and include all your skills, no matter how insignificant they may first appear.   After completing this exercise you will be able to use the information when preparing your Resume and highlight the matching skills to a potential employer during interview. The following is an example of how this could look:

SKILLS	KNOWLEDGE
Typing 60 w.p.m.	Filing systems
Forklift licence	Warehouse operations
Food and Beverage waiting	A la Carte service
Interviewing	Information gathering
Team leadership	Motivation techniques

Note the difference between identifying the SKILL and matching the associated KNOWLEDGE with that ability.   The SKILL can be more easily recognised and described as the TASK performed in any job and the KNOWLEDGE refers to the information you have which will enhance your ability to carry out the work.

STAY AT HOME PARENTS

Let's now use the Skills Audit process and look at what you may do unconsciously without being aware of the skill level required to carry out your daily routine. Stay-at-home parents are the equivalent to Managers in as much as they organise and co-ordinate automatically.

Here are a few examples of what is involved in running a home:

SKILLS	KNOWLEDGE
Time Management	Drawing up schedules
Prioritising	Recognising what needs to be done first
Networking	Who to contact socially, or in emergency
Co-ordinating people	Conducting meetings, running a trading table, organising tuck shop activities

These skills and associated knowledge go together, and can be used when assessing your competency in a particular area of employment. For example, during an interview you may be asked where your particular strengths lie, so it is important to be very familiar with the details in your Resume. You can then refer to the more successful functions you performed in previous work situations and use these examples as some of your strengths.

HOW LONG WILL IT TAKE?

Educational programs can take from several weeks as an introduction, to many years if you study on a part time basis. The standard qualification for many industries is Certificate III in "whatever field" (IT, Care Work, Hospitality etc). Some may be linked to a Traineeship; which is very useful because it virtually guarantees you employment for a year.

Certain jobs are not for everybody, but most people are good at most job once they get their own, and the jobs goals right.

The training you should look for should be comprehensive and presented by qualified trainers who all have current industry experience.

The educational methods and content should be;

- **current**
- **practical**
- **ethical**
- **skills and knowledge based**

Particular Occupations and jobs

Let's have a look at particular jobs, especially those in great demand at present.

A care-worker

In order to be a care-worker you will need to know how to;
- care for the hygiene of people
- Assist them with meals, bathing, dressing, grooming, communication and social needs.

- This means you will need to know how to do these tasks and know about safety. For example; how to transfer and lift people in and out of bed to the wheelchair.
- You may need to assist them if they have challenging behaviour or difficult episodes.
- You will need to ensure that whatever you do to assist people, you do it in the context of enhancing and maintaining their independence and assisting them to achieve a high quality of life.

As a care worker you must be able to provide for:
- the independence of people

- the mobility needs of people

- the personal care requirements of people

- the health requirements of people (including support with medication)

- the health and safety of people

- the special nutritional requirements of people

- The difficult behaviour people may have.

- the communication needs of people

- work with families

- facilitate rehabilitation of people

     and you must be able to

- contribute to team outcomes

- support community inclusion of people

Whilst all people you serve are different and all care workers have specific skills needs, these still remain the most commonly identifiable competencies a worker will require across the board and across the sector.

If you're considering becoming a "professional" care provider, you'll probably be aware that there is generally an abundance of work, and for those who are **"right"** for the job, will have that abundance of work. People who are not right for the job will be left disappointed. They will not get the hours they want and probably not even know why.

Workers who are trained and credentialled to Certificate III level are generally seen as capable of meeting a clients needs.

In summary

* **You must have the right <u>Attitudes</u> and <u>Values.</u>**
* **you must have the right <u>Skills</u>**
* **you must have the right <u>Knowledge</u>**

A hospitality worker

The hospitality industry, covers hotel managers, Waitress Jobs, Waiter Jobs, bartenders, chef jobs, kitchen staff, and hotel jobs. It has been growing fast, in Australia particularly in state capitals. It now accounts for one in 20 jobs in Australia, employing half a million people, making it a very attractive option. The industry also provides excellent opportunities for part-time and casual employment.

Most hospitality jobs like Bar Jobs and Waitress and Waiter Jobs in Australia do not require formal qualifications (apart from chef jobs and managerial positions), however many employers will be looking to hire staff with relevant experience and will also be looking for a certificate 11 or 111 in Hospitality or Retail, so make sure your resume is up-to-date and includes any relevant qualifications and references.

There is a huge range of jobs in the Australian hospitality industry in venues ranging from bars, restaurants and boutique hotels to multi-national hotels and entertainment venues like stadiums and theatres. Most backpackers work as bartenders or waiting staff, but there are is a wide range of hospitality jobs available in casual, permanent part-time, or full-time roles, such as:

- Bartenders and bar jobs in Australia in hotels, bars, café's and nightclubs

- Waiter/waitress jobs in restaurants and hotels

- Food preparation and service staff

- Function and corporate boardroom waitstaff

- Chef jobs — head chefs, sous chefs, chefs de partie etc

- Baristas

- Sommeliers

- Butlers, concierge, valet, and customer service roles roles

A lot of hospitality jobs, especially casual jobs, require you to work shifts ranging from three hours to seven or eight hours (or more). If you are a casual employee, you will work for an hourly rate. This can be a great way to earn money quickly because you can do plenty of hours/week and the hourly rate paid is higher then full time work.

In order to be a hospitality worker you will need to know how about (depending on your role);

- Dealing with colleagues and customers
- The Hospitality industry
- Workplace hygiene
- Accommodation reception services
- Bars and service of drinks
- Bottle shop operations and service
- Cafe/fast food operations
- Cellar operations
- Cleaning and maintaining kitchen premises
- Cleaning premises and equipment
- Clerical administration
- Club reception
- Espresso coffee service
- Food service procedures
- Gaming machine attending
- Housekeeping practices
- Housekeeping services

- Implementing food hygiene procedures
- Interpersonal communication and cultures
- Presenting food
- Receiving and storing kitchen supplies
- Removing waste
- Reservation procedures and service
- Responsible conduct of gambling
- Responsible service of alcohol
- Restaurant preparation and service
- Senior first aid

In addition some roles may require knowledge in;
- Bell desk/concierge
- Room service
- Hospitality financial transactions
- Hospitality products and services
- Cocktail service
- Maintaining clean storage
- Maintaining wet area
- Non alcoholic beverage service
- Organising and prepare food
- Preparing appetisers and salads
- Financial record keeping
- Front office practical
- Function service
- Keno
- Keyboarding - techniques and operations
- Laundry practices
- Preparing pastry cakes and yeast goods
- Preparing sandwiches
- Preparing stocks, sauces and soups
- Preparing vegetables, eggs and farinaceous
- Preparing, cook & serve food
- Silver service
- TAB overview
- Tourism & hospitality computing
- Valet/butler
- Wine and beverage service

Data adapted from Jobaroo Sydney, NSW 2060, Australia

An office worker

All organizations need timely and effective office and administrative support to operate efficiently. Office workers are employed in virtually every sector of the economy, working in positions varied positions from the junior clerk to the manager.

Although specific functions of office vary significantly, they share many common duties. You will be exposed to equipment and machinery used in various departments such as computer system photocopiers, fax machines

Office and administrative workers must understand and perform work such as;
- bookkeeping,
- accounting, and auditing
- cashier work
- interoffice communications work
- equipment operators
- customer service work
- data entry and information processing work
- general office work

- receptionist and information work
- stock and order work
- teller roles
- and much more.

Work environment.

Office and administrative support supervisors and managers are employed in a wide variety of work settings, but most work in clean and well-lit offices that usually are comfortable.

Most office and administrative workers, work a 38 hour week. However, some organizations operate around the clock, so some supervisors may have to work nights, weekends, and holidays. Sometimes, workers rotate among the three 8-hour shifts in a workday; in other cases, shifts are assigned on the basis of seniority.

In order to be an office worker you will need to know how to;

- provide customer service
- participate in data entry
- be able to operate as a general clerk
- provide typing and word processing
- listen and question to identify customer needs
- write customer notes, emails, faxes
- refer matters to nominated personnel
- work as a member of a team
- applying knowledge of one's own role to achieve team goals
- work with diverse persons and groups
- manage your own time and work priorities
- learn new ideas, skills and techniques
- adapt to new computerized systems, products and services
- use electronic communication devices and processes i.e. internet, intranet, telephony equipment, software packages, enterprise systems and email to action customer contact
- use technology to assist the manipulation of information
- work safely

Activity

What will you need to know next?

_____

_____

_____

_____

_____

_____

_____

_____

_____

_____

_____

_____

_____

_____

_____

_____

_____

COMPETENCIES & BASIC SKILLS YOU WILL NEED

SUMMARY OF BASIC SKILLS YOU WILL NEED

This is a broad guide to the basic competencies that are expected of a worker. You will need to take these on board and ensure that you have some or desirably all of them in order to be competitive in the job market.

In a nutshell you need to work with others, be able to get on, communicate well and do whatever your job is safely. Let's have a closer look...

Communication skills.
You are expected to communicate effectively and to be aware of the barriers to communicating clearly. You are expected to communicate with people with various disabilities as well as with people from non-English speaking backgrounds.

Teams skills.
You are expected to know about teamwork skills. You will need to know how to work with others in teams so as to effectively contribute to the team's outcomes. You are expected to know about workers roles and responsibilities within teams and how to get the best results out of working within a team.

Ability to Work safely
You will need to know about your roles and responsibilities in providing a safe working environment. You are expected to know about First Aid and have a knowledge of the emergency procedures tailored to your particular worksite.

Key Competencies
Although this is industry jargon which confuses and confounds many people, it is however important to navigate your way through unusual or foreign terminology in order for you to successfully obtain the work you are chasing.

A key competency refers to the set of skills and knowledge that underpin many jobs, such as your ability to use technology, work with others, organise yourself well and so on. Let's have a look at these in more detail, as it is a great guide for you to see what competencies you already have and what you may need to develop further.

Key Competency 1
The capacity to locate and use information...
It is important to be capable of working independently of others and demonstrate initiative by accessing information for use in your work

Key Competency 2
The capacity to communicate effectively with others...

This skill is essential if working in an area of customer service or any employment where you are dealing directly with the public. It is also required at all levels internally in any organisation where for example, you may have to report verbally to management meetings or instruct a fellow worker in any way.

Key Competency 3
The capacity to plan and organise one's work activities...
For just plain efficiency it is vital to be able to maintain an orderly workspace and prioritise your workload in a way that keeps things flowing

Key Competency 4
The capacity to interact effectively with other people...
People skills are highly valued no matter what industry or organisation you may apply for a position in and if well-developed, can be the difference between whether or not you are successful in you job search.

Key Competency 5
The capacity to use mathematical ideas...

Key Competency 6
The capacity to apply problem-solving strategies in purposeful ways...
This skill is highly sought after when an employer is looking for staff and it would be worthwhile developing at every opportunity so it can be included in your Resume, along with examples of where you used it successfully.

Key Competency 7
The capacity to apply technology...
Collecting, analyzing and organising information
".... The capacity to locate, sift and sort information in order to select what is required and presents it in a useful way. Evaluation can then be made of:
- the information itself
- the sources of the information and
- the methods used to obtain it

Key Competency 8
Communicating ideas and information
"...The capacity to effectively use the spoken language as well as a range of non-verbal methods of communication – i.e.
- written
- graphic
- body language

Key Competency 9
Planning and organising activities

"…. The capacity to plan and organise ones own work activities, including making good use of time and resources, sorting out priorities and monitoring ones own performance."

Key Competency 10
Working with others and in teams
"…. The capacity to interact effectively with other people both on a one-to-one basis and in groups, including understanding and responding to the needs of a client and working effectively as a member of a team to achieve a shared goal."

Key Competency 11
Using mathematical ideas and techniques
"…. The capacity to use mathematical ideas, such as number and space, and techniques, such as estimation and approximation, for practical purposes."

Key Competency 12
Solving Problems
"…. The capacity to apply problem solving strategies in purposeful ways, both in situations where the problems and the desired solution are clearly efficient and in situations requiring critical thinking and a creative approach to achieve an outcome."

Key Competency 13
Using technology
"…. The capacity to apply technology, combining the physical and sensory skills needed to operate equipment with the understanding of scientific and technological principles needed to explore and adapt systems."

Activity

What skills will you need?

_____

_____

_____

_____

_____

_____

_____

_____

_____

_____

_____

You will need to juggle many roles in your job

THERE'S MORE THAN ONE WAY TO GET WORK

THERE'S MORE THAN ONE WAY TO GET WORK

There are many ways to approach your task of getting work. Here are a few ways for you to consider. This list is by no means exhaustive. It is important that you keep your ears and eyes open for possibilities at all times if you want to be successful in landing a job quickly. Do not be afraid of knock backs. That is just a part of life, so get used to it and learn from every opportunity so you can improve your job hunting techniques.

* Look in the employment pages of the paper.

* Approach employers directly.

* Use private employment agencies or consultants.

* Talk to people who might know something.

* Check out professional and employer journals.

* The internet [e.g. job sites, direct to organisations, email response to your request]

The Employment Pages
One of the most obvious ways to look for work is to check the employment pages of the paper. As obvious as it may sound you would be surprised how many people actually don't bother to do this. Each state in Australia has its leading paper, so make sure you check them thoroughly and often. There are often many casual jobs you can apply for and I suggest you apply for as many as you can, if not all of them.

Direct Approach To Employers
You could visit, telephone or write to an employer even though you have not heard about a specific job vacancy. This is one of the most successful ways of getting a job.

Start by looking in the Yellow Pages for names of organisations that could use your particular skills. Obtain community services directories, and contact your local council to obtain a list of the employment agencies in your area, also check out employment services that specialise in contract labour hire.

Find out more about the agencies that attract you by asking what people around you know about the organisations, and ring them and ask them to send you information on their organisation.

Use these sources to get information you can use in your approach.
Some examples are;

- what the organisation does;
- what kind of training and experience they like their staff to have;
- if there are any new developments such as expansions to the service,
- The aims and philosophy of the organisation such as Consumer Focussed Service Delivery as a key philosophical platform.

You can then work out where your skills, interests and experience fit in. This information can then be used in writing your resume and in speaking to the employer. Then, either sends out copies of your resume with a covering letter asking for an interview, or calls in person and ask to see the human resource or recruitment officer of the organisation. You should take with you all the necessary papers such as *references and certificates* in case you are interviewed on the spot. If possible leave a copy of your resume to remind them of your visit. Follow up after a short while later with a telephone call or another personal visit. This method may mean visiting a large number of employers before you are successful.

Keep a record in a journal of all your contacts, the results and any follow up action, such as ringing or writing again, with a note of the date.

 Be patient. Remember, most people who gain work by this method do not get the job straight away, however they may be approached by the employer a few weeks or even months later. Persistence will pay off.

Private Employment Agencies
There are a number of private employment agencies that you can contact. Some may specialise in one or two occupational fields, or in several related fields, such as health care, personal care, catering, hospitality, accounting, engineering or secretarial and office work. Look for them under Employment Agencies in the Yellow Pages of the telephone book or through Centrelink.

Talk To People
Never limit your job search to advertised positions. They make up only a small proportion of the jobs available. Many vacancies are filled without ever being advertised. Remember that the unseen job market is far bigger than the advertised job market.

Talk to family members, friends, and relatives, past work mates and employers as sources of job leads. Most people are happy to give advice and help.

Professional / Employer Journals

Professional journals often carry job advertisements, and information on industries, which can prove useful in applications and interviews.

The journals are usually available in local libraries, college, university or State Libraries. Another library source is peak body agencies or large employers who may often have their own professional libraries.

<u>Using the Internet</u>

There are many advantages to using the Internet in looking for work, including the following:

- a wider employer audience
- greater job descriptions
- salary and award details ; including taxation information
- immediate access to the application process
- notification of employment opportunities for overseas travelers in Australia
- advice on schooling and vocational training

If you decide to take the opportunity to look for work using the Internet – be warned – each site will request Login identification. This can take some time, as it is difficult to find a unique Login name and password. Keep a written record of the different names and passwords used, as you will need to provide them each time you wish to enter the site.

(Handy Resources for Surviving Unemployment, "Using the Internet to Find a Job" p.27)

Activity

* Look in the employment pages of the paper.
* Approach employers directly.
* Use private employment agencies or consultants.
* Talk to people who might know something.
* Check out professional and employer journals.
* The internet
* Record what you have found here.

_____

_____

_____

_____

_____

_____

_____

_____

_____

_____

_____

_____

_____

_____

Always be on the look out!

WHAT TO DO WHEN APPLYING FOR WORK

WHAT TO DO WHEN APPLYING FOR WORK

Application Forms

Some employers require you to fill in an application form to apply for a job. The forms usually ask similar questions and there are some general points to follow.

- Read and follow the instructions carefully.

- Look through the form and think about each question before you start to fill in the answers.

- Answer all the relevant questions. If one doesn't apply to you write 'Not applicable' next to it.

- Always print neatly or have the form typed.

- Check your answers carefully to make sure they are correct.

Some Commonly Asked Questions

- **Position desired:** there may be more than one position available that you can apply for.

- **Health:** write 'good' unless you need to mention specific problems, which may affect this particular employment.

- **Past employment and reason for leaving:** if there is not enough space to list all you're past jobs, list only the latest and most relevant ones, or attach a separate page for the information. Be positive about your reason for leaving.

- **References:** list people who will give a good account of you're past work and personal qualities. Choose people who have responsible positions, and ask them first whether they will give you a supportive reference.

WHAT TO DO DURING A DOWNTURN OR RECESSION

At certain times in your lifetime you will experience economic and employment news which may be gloom and doom. You should not let it derail your hunt for work. You can still win a great job, even in a challenging economy. You WILL have to get smarter in your job search strategy, though, and you WILL need to stay away from a negative mindset.

Lets have a look at 5 steps to incorporate into your job search approach during difficult times such as a recession:

1. Research Your Options
Does the industry or line of work you have been used to offer little promise of employment in the coming months? If so, now is a good time to step back to identify the projected top performing industries and jobs. The best place to find this info is on the web through your browser. Start with "best industries work recession" or "recession jobs" to uncover articles and bloggs describing some of the more "recession-proof" sectors you could target. Having worked in the community services sector most of my life I can say with much certainty that if you become a carer, you WILL be in demand. In all my years I can reflect that we are always short staffed, and have to even go overseas (even now) to recruit. Whilst it may not be for everybody it's a great recession proofer, and later a gateway into many other jobs and professions.

2. Change Your Focus and stay Focused
Don't keep your old mind set of "what's in it for me"! Start asking yourself the question, "What's in it for *them*?" This is very important especially in an economic downturn; you'll want to stay focused on what you can accomplish for your next employer. Show them that you understand the "bigger picture" of the role you play in moving the organisation forward.

3. Sell *Results*, Not Skills
Leave behind that old mindset that your job-related skills or length of service are the only selling factors. The new mindset is to think of yourself as a mini enterprise rather than just an employee. Employers today like to buy ***results*** and are less impressed with candidates promoting a long list of skills and qualifications. You will want to define and highlight the many ways your past and present job performance are assets to your next employer.

4. Start Talking Money
The recession has made the private sector economy even more bottom-line oriented than ever. Managers and organizational leaders categorize employees into one of two distinct groups:

a.) staff who help make money

b.) staff who help save money.

Define which one you are

For example, Jamil worked as the human resources manager of a mid-sized organization. While much of his work focused on compliance issues, he noticed that the organization was paying many thousands of dollars to locate and hire good employees. As a result, he developed and implemented an in-house employee referral program that netted three quality hires in a six-month period. This saved the organization. Tens of thousands of dollars that the organization would have paid for recruiters and advertising costs.

Jamil **saves** money for his organization and this is an accomplishment future employers will want to hear about.

Rethink your current or past job to understand your position in the bigger organizational picture. Here are some questions to ask yourself:

- How did my work improve the performance or service of my organisation, business or section?

- How many roles did I perform that saved the organization the expense of added staff?

- How has my work made the work of others easier, faster and more effective?

Collect specific examples of the benefits that your organization gained from the work you've already performed. Clarify the specific benefit your organization received by making money or saving money, and write them down.

5. Add Achievements to Your Resume

I did not as many other employer hire employees, I hired *problem-solvers*. Your new resume should be a hard-hitting sales tool designed to accomplish one goal: **get the interview**. To demonstrate this, add a specific **achievements** list to your resume. Take the list that you developed in the previous section and hone it down to your biggest and most notable accomplishments. Now, describe the benefit that your employer gained from each example. This will put you several steps ahead of your job-seeking competitors. Plus, you'll now have some talking points ready for that next phone interview.

Take the time to tailor your resume to each application and make sure that you meet all of the requirements that are listed in the advertising in your resume and/or covering letter. Don't make them read between the lines and be explicit with it, or you'll risk blending in with thousands of other job seekers with similar skills. If you send a generic resume to every employer you end up being an average fit to everyone, and a great fit to no one.

Summary

Don't let all the hype about the recession spook you into a state of confusion, panic or apathy. By revising your tactics to include a more solution-selling approach to employers, you will be in a better position than many of getting work in a difficult economy.

Adapted from TURNER Job Hunting During the Recession?

 **Activity**

The next step is preparing your resume and your application letter.

Activity

What will you will need to do when applying for work during a downturn or a recession?

_____

_____

_____

_____

_____

_____

_____

_____

_____

_____

_____

_____

_____

_____

_____

_____

WRITTEN APPLICATIONS

WRITTEN APPLICATIONS

You can include details of your experience in a letter, or you can write an introductory letter and attach a resume. Both are acceptable although resumes are the norm.

Applying By Letter

The quality of your application will largely determine whether you obtain an interview. Possession of the necessary qualifications will not automatically guarantee an interview.

Your application should be made on good quality paper in clear writing, preferably typed and should include;

- reference to the position(s) applied for and the manner in which it (they) came to your attention; or reference to position(s) you are interested in within a particular organisation if the application is not in response to an advertised position
- your full name, address, telephone number
- educational and other qualifications
- details of any relevant employment experience (including vocational experience and voluntary work)
- copies of suitable references (or an indication that these can be provided)
- a brief statement of why you are interested in the position and that particular organisation
- your general career expectations

Close with an expression of your willingness to support your application at the interview.

As you may be applying for many positions, it is worthwhile compiling a resume (also called a curriculum vita) covering your experience and qualifications. (You should always send an introductory letter with the resume, in which you refer to the position you are applying for and highlight your particular qualifications for the position and your interest in the job.

A cover or introductory letter

Contact Information

The first section of your cover letter should include information on how the employer can contact you. If you have contact information for the employer, include that. Otherwise, just list your information.

- Your Name
- Your Address
- Your City, State, Code
- Your Phone Number
- Your Email Address
- Date

Employer Contact Information

- Name
- Title
- Company
- Address
- City, State, Code

Salutation

- Dear Mr./Ms. Last Name:

Body of Cover Letter

The body of your cover letter lets the employer know what position you are applying for, why the employer should select you for an interview, and how you will follow-up.

First Paragraph:

The first paragraph of your letter should include information on why you are writing. Mention the position you are applying for. Include the name of any mutual contact, if you have one. Ensure you are clear and concise regarding your request.

Middle Paragraphs:

The next section of your cover letter should describe what you have to offer the employer. Convince the reader that they should grant the interview or appointment you requested in the first paragraph. Make strong connections between your abilities and their needs. Mention specifically how your skills and experience match the job you are applying for. Remember, you are **interpreting** your resume, not repeating it. Try to support each statement you make with a piece of evidence. Use several shorter paragraphs or bullets rather than one large block of text.

Final Paragraph:

Conclude your cover letter by thanking the employer for considering you for the position. Include information on how you will follow-up. State that you will do so and indicate when (one week's time is typical). You may want to reduce the time between sending out your resume and follow up if you fax or e-mail it.

Complimentary Close:

- Respectfully yours,

Signature:

- Handwritten Signature for a mailed letter
- Typed Signature

Activity

Start your draft here.

_____

_____

_____

_____

_____

_____

_____

_____

_____

_____

_____

_____

_____

_____

_____

_____

_____

_____

A resume is;

An assessment of your labour market potential.

It is a summary of facts describing your academic or professional training, activities and any job experience you have had.

Above all, it reflects what you have accomplished and its purpose is to prove that you are capable of doing the job you seek.

RESUME PREPARATION

NO ONE IS INTERESTED IN

WHAT YOU WANT

UNTIL YOU CREATE

INTEREST IN

WHAT YOU CAN OFFER

THEM

REMEMBER,
YOUR RESUME IS A
ONE MINUTE OPPORTUNITY
TO CONVINCE OTHERS OF YOUR
ABILITIES
TO SOLVE THEIR PROBLEMS

THE NEXT
STEP

THE NEXT STEP

The next step in the job seeking process is to ensure that you have developed a Resume that you can submit with your letter of application.

You need a Resume because:

1. It gives you the opportunity to sell yourself - to list all those qualities that make you a suitable applicant for a job.

2. Preparing a Resume gives you a clear picture of your talents and qualifications for employment. It makes it easier for you to write relevant applications.

3. A Resume gives an employer an immediate picture of your potential as an employee.

Your Resume only gets 15-20 seconds of reading time. You get one chance to make a good first impression.

When you think about sending a Resume to an Employer, keep one thought in mind, that the organisation is asking

"What can you do for us?"

You can't be there to answer the question, so your Resume must speak for you.

For a moment, consider the traditional opening question in a job interview. "Tell us about yourself"... If it's important, and you think that the employer should know, make sure you include it in your Resume.

You must know what is in your Resume backwards, because the employer may question you about the contents.

WHAT IS A RESUME?

- A brief history of your related skills and abilities.

- It outlines your personal details, education and work experience.

- It might also contain other relevant information – interests and hobbies.

THE PURPOSE OF A RESUME

A resume is designed to present information about your work history and related skills to an employer as evidence of your suitability for a vacancy.

WHY MUST IT LOOK GOOD

A resume is like an advertisement. If the ad is good we are inclined to look at the product, if not we tend to ignore it. The same is true for the resume. If it is presented well an employer is more likely to move to the next stage and invite you to an interview.

When preparing your resume make sure that it:

- Is easy to read – have lots of white space
- Is neat and tidy
- Is free of spelling and grammatical errors
- Have section headings

No matter how careful you are there is always the possibility of mistakes so ask someone else to proof read your resume before you send it off.

IS ONE RESUME ENOUGH?

Generally speaking it is OK to prepare one resume and use this for any job you are after. If you choose to do this then your covering letter will need to refer the points contained in the job and person specification. Some people however decide to prepare a resume which is adapted for each of the different positions they are applying for. There is no right or wrong way to go on this point. It comes down to personal preference.

WHAT DOES A RESUME CONTAIN?

Every resume should contain the following essential sections:

- *Personal Details*
- *Education*
- *Employment History or Work Experience*

Everything else is optional and what you include will depend on the position you have applied for or your situation.

Personal Details

- Your name –Include your full first name not just initials.
- Your address –Write your full postal address
- Your phone number – Include day and after hours numbers and a fax number if you have one. If you do not have a phone, see if you can include the number of someone who can contact you quickly, just in case the employer wants to set up an interview quickly.

No other information is required. Details like marital status, health age disability etc. are not important and should not be included, as they have no relevance to the work you will be doing.

Education

Start with your most recent qualification and move backwards to your earliest qualification. Your final school qualification is far enough.

List the date first followed by the qualification, name of institution and where it is located.

If your qualification is general and you specialise in a particular area, or if the interviewer might not understand how it is relevant to the job, give extra detail to make it clear.

Employment History

When you have had little work experience, it makes sense to put your educational achievements first. If you think your employment history is the strongest reason for getting a job put that first?

For a basic work history you must show the

- Date

- Position title

- Name and location of the company you worked for

There are a number of different ways you can provide extra information. For each position you could describe the tasks you accomplished and your duties and responsibilities. This is useful because the person interviewing you may not understand the skills required undertaking that particular job unless you explain them.

This information can be listed under a subheading - **responsibilities.**

If you wish, for each position you may also wish to list any specific work related achievements, for example, service awards, major projects, or work undertaken outside the range of your job description. List these under a subheading – **achievements.**

Listing your work history:
You may list work history by date or by type.

Date: Arrange your examples of employment in order of date from the most recent to earliest job.

Type: You could arrange your jobs into groupings, with similar jobs under descriptive headings. This is useful if you have had a lot of experience, or have had a number of jobs in different fields.

When you **don't have much experience**, you need to give full descriptions of all part time and any unpaid work you may have had. You should emphasize the relationship between the responsibilities of these jobs and the one you are applying for.

When your **work history is not continuous** and there are large gaps, give the interviewer some indication of what might have been doing during this time.

Example: domestic duties travelled extensively, caring for invalid relative, study etc.

When **you have worked without being paid** list it as you would a job, showing the date and place and what you're main duties and responsibilities were.

The following categories are optional and whether or not you use them will be very much an individual choice. Use them only if they are relevant to the job you are applying for and will improve your chances of obtaining an interview.

- Other work skills
- Community activities
- Sporting activities
- Other interests
- Hobbies

Referees and References

On your resume you can include the names of two referees who can recommend you to an employer. Who you choose will again depend on the nature of the job you are applying for. Choose people who can discuss your work performance. If this is not possible select people like teachers or others who may have observed the application of skills that you claim to possess. Make sure you include names and contact numbers as well as addresses for each one.

Use personal or character references only if these are requested or you do not have an alternative.

 **Activity**

Start notes on:
- *Personal Details*

_____

_____

_____

_____

_____

_____

_____

_____

_____

 **Activity**

Start notes on:
- *Education*

_____

_____

_____

_____

_____

_____

Activity

Start notes on:
- *Employment History or Work Experience*

_____

_____

_____

_____

_____

_____

_____

_____

When producing your Resume you need to:

1. Include all relevant details under major headings (if possible target your Resume for the job by including key words from the advertisement / job specification).

2. Have it typed, well spaced and neatly set out in point form. Make it look professional.

3. Ensure that there are no typing, spelling or grammatical errors.

4. Keep it brief and to the point.

5. Don't think of it as a list of facts, it should also be a Resume of your personal, educational and career history, as well as an indication of your individual strengths and achievements.

Remember your resume is an advertisement of you

Constructing a Resume

On the following page you will find a program Resume as a guide for your use.

REMEMBER:

Keep in mind "what are they looking for?" and only include job-related information. Ensure that this information is displayed in the order that an employer will consider the most important.

Only include information, which shows your ability to do a job. If information isn't job related, it doesn't belong in your Resume.

For some people it's hard to keep focused in this way. They want to display everything that they have to offer which often isn't relevant to the job they are applying for. The reader will lose interest and instead of keeping your Resume on the file, it's placed in the waste paper bin instead.

Activity

Personal notes on:

_____

_____

_____

_____

_____

_____

_____

_____

A resume should allow a prospective employer to gain a good impression of what you can offer by way of skills, experience and personal qualities. It is the gateway to an interview and is therefore a very valuable tool in job searching. If a resume does not contain all the important facts, then you are letting yourself down before you start.

Turn to the next page and study the pro forma Resume provided for you. It has been designed to cover the major areas of information required to complete a successful Resume. Please fill this out thoughtfully, taking care to put in dates wherever possible - not forgetting STD and postcodes. Every person is different and has different strengths and experience, so some sections may not be relevant to you - if so, just leave them blank. Write clearly, especially for names.

You may be surprised by the end of this exercise and may look at yourself in a different light when you see just how many positives there are to say about yourself.

Activity

Use the résumé pro-forma to help you construct your resume.

RESUME PRO FORMA

NAME
(Full name - title optional, e.g.; Ms, Mr., Mrs., Miss)

ADDRESS;
(No. Of the place, street name, suburb, state, postcode)

TELEPONE
Home   or Contact No for Message;

DATE OF BIRTH; (optional)

MARITAL STATUS; (optional)

HEALTH; (optional)
(If non-smoker - say so)

DRIVERS LICENCE;
(Give details of class and type-e.g. light truck, heavy truck, forklift etc. and whether you have your own transport)

PERSONAL QUALITIES AND STRENGTHS

List positive personality traits, e.g. reliable, willing to learn, creative etc. as well as what you are good at and any special abilities; e.g. working in a group / alone / unsupervised, language skills, working with children.

SPECIFIC ACHIEVEMENTS

Add a specific **achievements** list to your resume of your biggest and most notable accomplishments, such as how many roles you can perform, how in your last role you made the work of others easier, faster and more effective, specific examples of the benefits that your organization gained from your past work.

WORK SKILLS ACQUIRED

Include any skills learned during previous jobs, work experience, voluntary works and courses.)

EQUIPMENT USED

(Include any machines used, lifting or health care devices office equipment.)

ADDITIONAL TRAINING

(Give details of any courses since leaving school- showing dates, where, what course, what topics/subjects covered and any certificates and qualifications gained.)

ENSURE YOU WRITE IT IN REVERSE CHRONOLOGICAL ORDER

EXAMPLE;

Date	Jul-Dec 1999
Where	Enable College for Carers
Course	Community Services And Health Certificate 3
Subjects	Identifying Client Needs, Recognising and Supporting Client Rights, Supporting Difference and Diversity, Health Care Needs of the Older Person, Duty of Care, Independent Personal Care, Meal Time Management, Maintaining Safe Workplace, Observation and Reporting,
Qualifications	Gained Certificate -

Date
Where
Course
Subjects
Qualifications

Date
Where
Course
Subjects
Qualifications

EDUCATION

(Include details of any special awards or achievements.)
ENSURE YOU WRITE IT IN REVERSE CHRONOLOGICAL ORDER

DATES
SCHOOL
YEAR LEVEL
SUBJECTS

ACHIEVEMENTS

EMPLOYMENT HISTORY

ENSURE YOU WRITE IT IN REVERSE CHRONOLOGICAL ORDER

EXAMPLE

DATE	12/3/92 - 14/4.2003
WHERE	Enable Care Services
POSITION HELD	Care Worker
DUTIES	Provision of personal care and assistance to elderly people and support with activities of daily living.

DATE
WHERE
POSITION HELD
DUTIES

DATE
WHERE
POSITION HELD
DUTIES

DATE
WHERE
POSITION HELD
DUTIES

WORK EXPERIENCE

(This section only needs to be filled in if you have any of this type of experience.)

DATE
WHERE
TYPE OF SERVICE
DUTIES

DATE
WHERE
TYPE OF SERVICE
DUTIES

VOLUNTARY WORK

(This section only needs to be filled in if you have any of this type of experience.)

DATE
WHERE
DUTIES

COMMUNITY AND LEISURE ACTIVITIES/INTERESTS

(Give details of any community involvement's, sporting clubs, scouts etc. as well as other interests, e.g. bushing walking, photography, surfing -only major ones.)

CAREER OBJECTIVE

(What you would like to do in your work-life, make a statement here.)

REFEREES

(Provide a total of three people who can be contacted by an employer.
You will need to write down the FULL NAME, POSITION HELD, ADDRESS AND PHONE NUMBER. It is helpful to distinguish between Professional and Personal Referees.)

Professional Referee

Name
Position
Company
Address

Ph (   )

Professional
Referee

Name
Position
Company
Address

Ph (   )

Academic Referee

Name
Position
Institution
Address

Ph (   )

Personal
Referee

Name
Other Details

Address

Ph (   )

THE INTERVIEW

THE INTERVIEW

Physical appearance

This is the stage where you need to present your physical appearance well, ensuring you are well dressed and groomed and are mentally alert to the possible interview questions.

- Clothes to wear
- Hair
- Facial hair
- Make up
- Shoes
- Personal care
- Your posture

Introductions

When you first meet the interviewer(s) ensure you send positive signals as soon as you make eye contact. This can be in the form of a smile, eye contact, demonstrating you are confident in yourself. Introduce yourself and shake hands firmly but not roughly. Let the interviewer start the dialogue and take your cue from them.

Find out about the job

Takes the time prior to the interview to do some research on the history and purpose of the organisation you are applying to. Then, find out about the job by listening intently. Ask relevant questions, as there is no point in pursuing a job that isn't right for you.

Interview Questions

Whether there is a panel of interviewers or just one, there will always be questions asked of you. The employer wants to know if you have the knowledge and skills to do the job. There are many combinations possible and below I have listed a few you may start to think about.

Adapted from Tamara Dowling 2000-09

- Tell me about yourself.
- Of which personal accomplishments are you most proud?
- What are your strengths?
- What are your weaknesses?
- Could you outline for us your relevant skills, qualifications and experience that you think you can offer this position.
- Could you tell us about your experience working in this industry or your reasons for being interested in this position.
- How do you see your role / responsibility in keeping the work area safe?
- What do you see as being the effective elements of teamwork?
- Tell me about a conflict with a co-worker. How did you handle it?
- Tell me about a disagreement with your current or previous Supervisor. How did you handle it?
- How do you react to negativity or gossip from co-workers?
- If you found out a co-worker was/is dishonest, what would you do?
- If you were unable to meet a commitment or deadline, what would you do?
- Tell me about your best Supervisor, and why you regard them that way.
- Tell me about your worst Supervisor, and why you regard them this way? Note: Remember the rule about saying nothing negative about past employers and associates. *This may tempt you, but it is best to say that you've learned something from all of your Supervisors.*
- Describe your toughest problem and how you handled it. Note: Focus on accomplishments, and do not blame or say anything negative about your associates.
- If a customer is disrespectful to you, what do you do?
- If you were unable to resolve a customer issue by the date promised because another department did not do its job, what would you do, and what would you say to the customer?
- What makes you the best candidate?
- Do you prefer to work alone or in a group?
- Tell me about your organization/time management style.
- How well do you work with multiple people or vendors?
- Describe a project that you managed. Was the project completed on time and on/under budget? Why/Why not? What would you have done differently?
- Describe how you motivate your staff or fellow team members.
- How would your staff or team members describe you?
- How would your current Supervisor describe you?
- Where do you want to be in five years?
- Why do you want this job? Note: Focus on benefits to the company and how your skills and goals fit the company's needs and goals.

Answer all the questions honestly and if you are not clear on what has been asked, ask the interviewer to repeat the question. If you are nervous, it may be worthwhile acknowledging that to the interviewer. They are not heartless and generally understand.

During the interview
During the interview make sure you convey the right messages such as

* you are willing to work

* you are keen to learn

* you are flexible

* you will contribute to the organisation

When the interview is finished makes sure you have a couple of good questions and wait for your cue to finish off.

Waiting for results

Waiting for the results of an interview can be a frustrating time for you so the strategy I recommend is that you put your energy into;

* applying for more jobs
* attending more interviews
* gaining more skills while you wait

Get Feedback! Receiving a response from the interview

You may receive a response either by mail or phone or both. It may be that you were successful, so your new employer will give you instructions and you will need to follow them closely. If you are not clear on the next step then make sure you clarify it or you will get off to a bad start.

If you are not successful at **that** time, then you don't have the luxury to be negative about it. What your task is now, is to find out from the interviewer what it was that precluded you from getting the job at this time. This is so you can make sure that you will make the necessary adjustments for next time. If you fail to learn, from each interview you plan to fail more often. That is not in your plan is it? It is also useful to listen to positive feedback. A professional interviewer will almost certainly give you feedback on what you did well.

...If you fail to learn from each interview, You plan to fail more often...

Remember getting a job in this field is not difficult if you have;

- the right **A**ttitude

- the right **S**kills

- the right **K**nowledge

Key Principles of Workplace Dress Code

Personal presentation requirements for business activities.

Key Principles

- Neat comfortable business clothing

- Care with your personal hygiene, hair neat and tidy

- No fashion extremes

- Demonstrate success and be a role model to our clients through business dress

- Being sensitive to particular cultural dress requirements

While casual dress may be more comfortable and practical. There are some who still believe that a more formal approach is best, and that a suit and tie is necessary for business tasks—such as meeting customers, trips to clients, and working side by side with others in business.

Appropriate Dress
Neat comfortable business clothing such as shirt, tie (optional), jumper or business jacket is generally considered appropriate.

Heavy jackets e.g., leather parkas; trench coats should not be used during work as it presents a contrary image we wish to portray. Etc.

Ensure all your garments are clean and fresh. Clothes carry stale smells quite readily so ensure they are clean and aired regularly.

For front line Staff
Front-line staff are those who interact with the public as part of their job.

Business dress should include business clothing such as shirt, tie (optional), jumper or business jacket is generally considered appropriate. Our corporate colours are black, although not mandatory; these are the themes we aspire to.

Personal Hygiene
Extra care with your personal hygiene (clothing, hair and deodorant etc) is required when working in close proximity with others. If you have been undertaking strenuous activities we are happy to provide a deodorant cologne or alike for business use.

Employees should regularly trim beards, moustaches and keep hair clean and tidy.

Tattoos are not banned however; their display should be minimized.

The wearing of earrings and other jewellery to both men and women is acceptable providing it does not follow fashion extremes.

Personal presentation requirements and Uniforms

Many jobs such as hospitality staff, carers, nurses, technicians may be required to wear particular uniforms or styles of clothing. Check to see what requirements you may need to comply with. Some simple observations of people already working in the industry will generally give you this information.

Activity

- What do I need to focus on?

_____

_____

_____

_____

_____

_____

_____

_____

_____

_____

_____

_____

_____

_____

_____

EMPLOYMENT OPPORTUNITIES

DONT FORGET TO CONTACT;

* **Hotels**
* **Motels**
* **Café chains**
* **All Local Councils**
* **Community Care Programmes**
* **Nursing Homes**
* **Retirement Villages/Hostels**
* **Information Centres**
* **The Internet**
* **Government Sites**

Now that you have obtained the above resources decide which places you will apply for first. To help organize yourself you may wish to list them on the chart below. Start making contact with these places and sending your resume to those organizations that show an interest. In the first week I usually send out about five resumes. Then the following week I contact them to gauge their interest. If interest is low I send out another five resumes to different organizations. I then repeat the process the following week. Be prepared to attend some interviews at any time and ensure you are contactable at all times. It's no good sending out resumes when they can't contact you to offer you an interview. If your success is low then continue this process of resume sending and follow up. If you continue to have no results then you'll need to look at the quality of your resume and the manner in which you approach the employer when you are talking with them over the phone.

Activity

Brainstorm all the possible places you could apply for. Put them in categories such as; hotels, shops, or nursing homes etc.

Category 1

_____

_____

_____

_____

_____

_____

_____

Activity

Category 2

_____

_____

_____

_____

_____

_____

_____

_____

Activity

Category 3

_____

_____

_____

_____

_____

_____

Activity

Category 4

_____

_____

_____

_____

_____

_____

_____

_____

Activity

Category 5

_____

_____

_____

_____

_____

_____

_____

Now start on your shopping list on the next page.

My Job Shopping List

Name of service	Address	Phone number	Date sent
E.g.... Anglican Community Services	16 King William Road NORTH ADELAIDE SA 5006	8239 8200	
Café Primo			
Café Buono			
Central Market			
Aussie Mining Co.			
Australian Defence Force			
Safeway Security Service			
Aged Care Services Aus			
Apples are Us			
Lawn Mowing for U			

ADD TO THIS LIST AND KEEP IT UP TO DATE

Work in the regional or rural districts

My advice to people looking for work in the country is to find country community services directories, contact the council offices and check out employment services that specialise in contract labour hire.

APPENDIX / NOTES

On Line / videos

Improve Your Interview Appearance and Body Language
with Alison Doyle
http://video.about.com/jobsearch/Job-Interview-Body-Language.htm

Phone Interview Tips
with Alison Doyle
http://video.about.com/jobsearch/Job-Interview-Body-Language.htm

Improve Your Interview Appearance and Body Language
with Alison Doyle
http://video.about.com/jobsearch/Job-Interview-Body-Language.htm

Books

Richard Bolles; **What Color Is Your Parachute?** A Practical Manual for Job-Hunters and Career-Changers. 2009 edition Ten Speed Press.

Handy Resources for Surviving Unemployment; SEMYA NEWS

TURNER; **Job Hunting During the Recession?** 2009